# NIGHTMARE PLAGUES

# THE FLU OF 1918
## Millions Dead Worldwide!

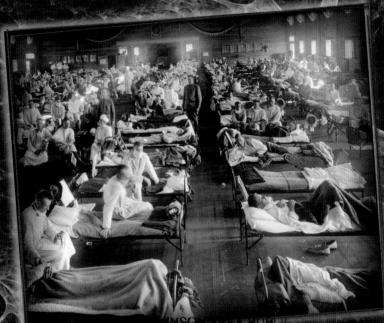

## by Jessica Rudolph

Consultant: Dr. Marc Strassburg
Adjunct Professor
Department of Epidemiology, UCLA;
Professor, Health Sciences
TUI University

## BEARPORT
### PUBLISHING

New York, New York

## Credits

Cover and Title Page, © Courtesy of The National Museum of Health and Medicine; 4, Courtesy of Donald Jacobi; 4–5, Courtesy of The National Museum of Health and Medicine; 7, © Edward A. "Doc" Rogers, Joseph R. Knowland Collection, Oakland History Room, Oakland Public Library; 8, © Karsten Schneider/Science Photo Library/Photo Researchers, Inc.; 9T, © Corbis/SuperStock; 9B, © silverlining56/iStockphoto; 10, © Scott Camazine/Alamy; 11L, © Rue des Archives/The Granger Collection, New York; 11R, Courtesy of The Newspaper Archive; 13, Courtesy of the U.S. Naval History and Heritage Command; 14L, © Wellcome Library, London; 14R, © Harris & Ewing, Inc./ Corbis; 15, Courtesy of The Library of Congress; 16, © Illustrated London News Ltd/Mary Evans Picture Library; 17L, Courtesy of The National Archives at College Park, MD; 17R, Courtesy of The Samuel Paley Library Temple University Libraries, Urban Archives, Philadelphia, Pennsylvania; 18, © Museum of History & Industry/Zuma Press/ Newscom; 19, Courtesy of The Philadelphia Archdiocesan Historical Research Center; 20, © Bettmann/Corbis; 21T, © Time Life Pictures/National Archives/Time Life Pictures/Getty Images; 21B, © Courtesy of National Archives at College Park, MD; 22T, © Underwood & Underwood/Corbis; 22B, © Bettmann/Corbis; 23, © Bettmann/Corbis; 24L, © image100/SuperStock; 24R, © Feature China/Newscom; 25, © Ralf Hirschberger/Deutsche Presse-Agentur/ Newscom; 26L, © Sebastian Kaulitzki/Shutterstock; 26R, © Gu Jun/ChinaFotoPress/Getty Images; 27, © Zuma Press/Newscom; 28T, Courtesy of The National Museum of Health and Medicine; 28B, © Bettmann/Corbis; 29, © U.S. Centers for Disease Control/MCT/Newscom; 31, © Frances M. Roberts/Irphotos/Newscom.

Publisher: Kenn Goin
Editorial Director: Adam Siegel
Creative Director: Spencer Brinker
Design: Dawn Beard Creative
Photo Researcher: Picture Perfect Professionals, LLC

*Library of Congress Cataloging-in-Publication Data*

Rudolph, Jessica.
 The flu of 1918 : millions dead worldwide! / by Jessica Rudolph.
   p. cm. — (Nightmare plagues)
 Includes bibliographical references and index.
 ISBN-13: 978-1-936088-05-8 (library binding)
 ISBN-10: 1-936088-05-3 (library binding)
 1. Influenza Epidemic, 1918-1919—Juvenile literature. I. Title.
 RC150.4.R83 2011
 614.5'1809041—dc22
                    2010004684

For more information, write to Bearport Publishing Company, Inc., 101 Fifth Avenue, Suite 6R, New York, New York 10003. Printed in the United States of America in North Mankato, Minnesota.

062010
042110CGB

10 9 8 7 6 5 4 3 2 1

# Contents

Not the Normal Flu ........................ 4

"He'll Be Dead by Morning" ................... 6

Tiny Invaders ................................ 8

War Helps Spread the Flu ................... 10

Influenza Explodes in America .............. 12

Scary Symptoms ........................... 14

Trying to Stop a Killer ..................... 16

Reminders of Death and Disease............ 18

Young Victims.............................. 20

A Lasting Impact........................... 22

Help from Vaccines ....................... 24

A New Flu ................................. 26


Other Famous Flu Outbreaks ................. 28

Flu Facts ....................................... 29

Glossary ....................................... 30

Bibliography.................................... 31

Read More...................................... 31

Learn More Online ............................ 31

Index .......................................... 32

About the Author ............................. 32

# Not the Normal Flu

It was a fall day in 1918 when Donald Jacobi came home sick from school in South Buffalo, New York. The five-year-old had a high **fever**. Donald's parents were fairly certain that their son had **influenza**, or the flu. People with the flu feel very sick for a few days. However, they usually get better soon. Unfortunately, this was no ordinary flu.

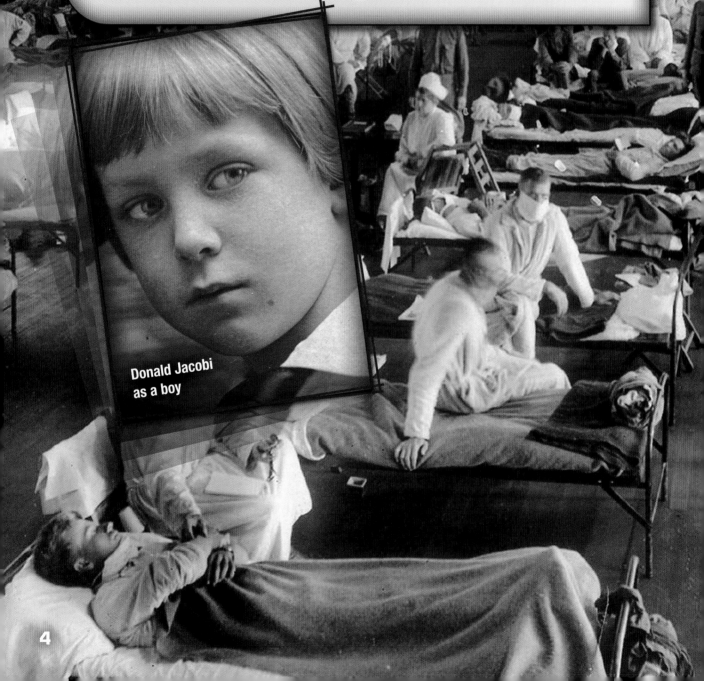

Donald Jacobi as a boy

Donald's fever didn't go down over the next few days, so his parents called a doctor to check on him. The doctor told Donald's parents to take their son to the hospital right away.

When the family reached the hospital, however, they were told they couldn't come inside. Other patients might catch what Donald had. Instead, the sick boy had to go to a nearby building called the "pesthouse"—a place where flu patients were sent to die.

All of the patients crowded into this hospital in 1918 are sick with the flu.

People with the flu can get headaches, chills, a fever, achy muscles, a cough, sore throat, and feel extremely weak.

# "He'll Be Dead by Morning"

Donald's mother, Magdalena, asked a doctor in the pesthouse for help. "There's nothing we can do for him," he said. "He'll be dead by morning." Magdalena replied, "If he's going to die, he's going to die at home."

The family brought Donald to their car and began the drive back to their house. During the ride, Donald's health got worse. The five-year-old became **unconscious**. It seemed as though he might soon be dead.

QUARANTINE

INFLUENZA

By Order of BOARD OF HEALTH

Blake D. Johnfellow

KEEP OUT OF THIS HOUSE          HEALTH OFFICER

The flu spreads quickly and easily between people. When Donald was sick, the Jacobis put a quarantine sign outside their home to warn friends and neighbors to stay away because they could catch the disease.

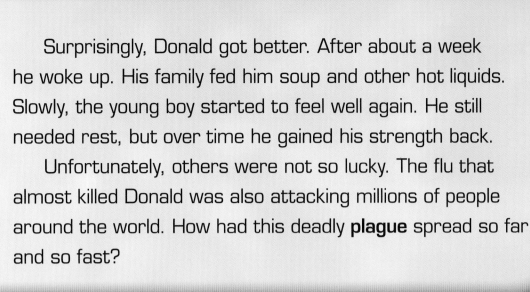

Surprisingly, Donald got better. After about a week he woke up. His family fed him soup and other hot liquids. Slowly, the young boy started to feel well again. He still needed rest, but over time he gained his strength back.

Unfortunately, others were not so lucky. The flu that almost killed Donald was also attacking millions of people around the world. How had this deadly **plague** spread so far and so fast?

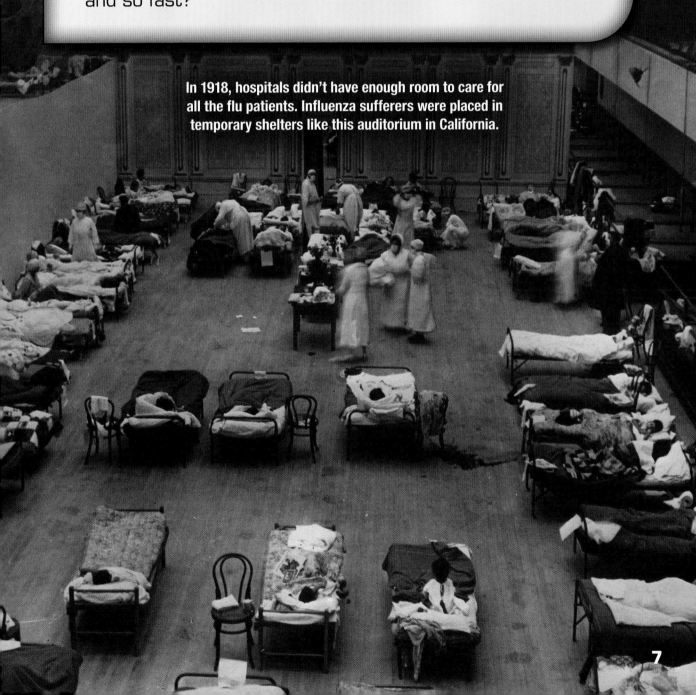

In 1918, hospitals didn't have enough room to care for all the flu patients. Influenza sufferers were placed in temporary shelters like this auditorium in California.

# Tiny Invaders

Influenza **infections**, including the one that attacked Donald, are caused by **viruses**. These are small germs that cause diseases. A flu virus enters a person's body when he or she breathes it in.

After entering a person, the virus **invades** one of the **cells** that make up the body, such as a lung cell. The virus then makes thousands of copies of itself. Viruses destroy the cell by breaking out of it. Next, they look for other cells to invade and kill.

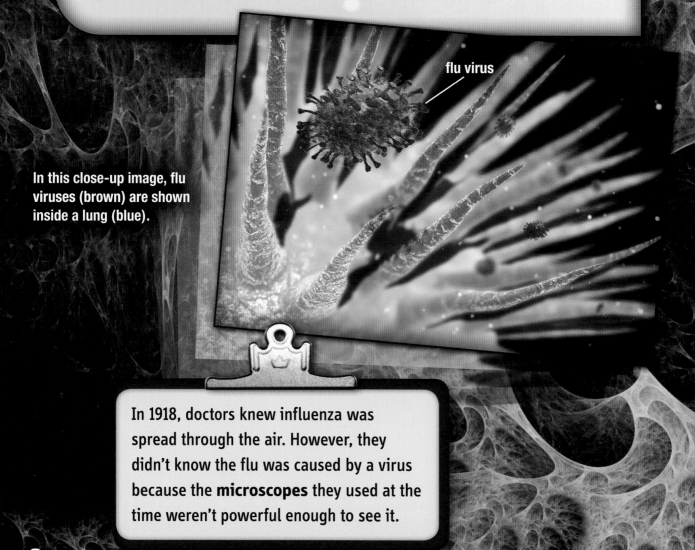

flu virus

In this close-up image, flu viruses (brown) are shown inside a lung (blue).

In 1918, doctors knew influenza was spread through the air. However, they didn't know the flu was caused by a virus because the **microscopes** they used at the time weren't powerful enough to see it.

Luckily, human bodies have white blood cells, which surround and destroy viruses. They also have proteins, which make a body strong. One kind of protein, called an **antibody**, grabs on to viruses and stops them from moving through the body. Usually, white blood cells and antibodies can easily fight off flu viruses. However, the 1918 flu was stronger than most flu viruses.

Part of the sick feeling a flu sufferer gets, like a sore throat, is from the damage the virus does to the body's cells.

The flu virus spreads easily from person to person when someone breathes, coughs, or sneezes. It can also spread when a person touches an object with flu germs on it, such as a doorknob, and then touches his or her nose or mouth.

# War Helps Spread the Flu

The 1918 influenza virus spread quickly. It probably first appeared in an army camp in Kansas. On the morning of March 11, 1918, a soldier went to the camp hospital with a fever, sore throat, and a headache. By noon, 100 more flu patients had arrived at the hospital. By the end of the week, there were 500 flu cases.

The flu virus can live in the body for a few days before a person starts feeling sick. However, people can't spread the virus until they start to have **symptoms**, such as coughing and sneezing.

This photo shows how far flu germs can spread in the air when people don't cover their mouths when they sneeze.

That spring and summer, 1.5 million American soldiers, including some from Kansas, were shipped to Europe. They went to fight in World War I (1914–1918). Unfortunately, many of them were infected with the flu virus. As a result, thousands more American soldiers got sick in Europe. They then spread the deadly influenza to English, Spanish, French, and German soldiers—just by breathing.

Soon the flu was a **pandemic**. Millions of **civilians** in several European countries began to get sick. As people who carried the virus traveled, it spread to Asia, Africa, and other areas. By late summer, the flu was a worldwide crisis.

The 1918 flu is sometimes called the Spanish influenza because Spain was one of the first countries that had many deaths due to the flu.

## SPANISH INFLUENZA--A NEW NAME FOR AN OLD FAMILIAR DISEASE

Simply the Same Old Grip That Has Swept Over the World Time and Again—The Last Epidemic in the United States Was in 1889-90.

**ORIGIN OF THE DISEASE.**
Spanish Influenza, which appeared in Spain in May, has swept over the world in numerous epidemics as far back as history runs. Hippocrates refers to an epidemic in 412 B. C.

heat of the body liberates the ingredients in the form of vapors. These vapors, inhaled with each breath carry the medication directly to the parts affected. At the same time VapoRub is absorbed through and

During World War I, millions of soldiers lived and fought in close quarters, which made it easy for the flu to spread.

# Influenza Explodes in America

In the United States, the flu **outbreak** didn't spread beyond army camps—until September 3, 1918. On that day, the first American civilian got sick in Boston, Massachusetts. By October 1, there were more than 75,000 flu cases in the state.

## How the 1918 Flu Spread Across America

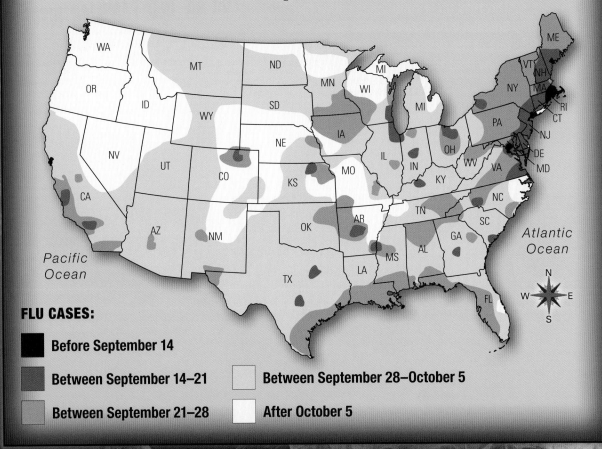

**FLU CASES:**

- Before September 14
- Between September 14–21
- Between September 21–28
- Between September 28–October 5
- After October 5

In a few weeks, from September to October 1918, the flu virus spread across the United States from the East Coast to the West Coast.

Other Americans heard about what was happening in Massachusetts. They knew the disease would reach them soon—and they were right. One of the places that was hit the hardest was Philadelphia, Pennsylvania. On September 28, more than 200,000 people went to see a parade in the city. The flu virus spread quickly through the crowds.

A week later, on October 5, about 250 people died of the flu in Philadelphia. The next day, another 289 died. The number of daily deaths kept rising. In one single day, October 16, more than 700 people died. Some people feared that the flu would kill everyone.

October 1918 is the month in which the most people died in U.S. history—more than 195,000 people were killed by influenza.

On September 28, 1918, the city of Philadelphia held a parade to raise money for the war in Europe. Many people caught the flu while attending this parade.

# Scary Symptoms

Flu viruses come in different strains, or types. The strain that spread in 1918 was very powerful. It caused horrible symptoms. Some people had such bad body aches that it felt like their bones were breaking. For others, their lungs filled up with so much bloody fluid that blood even came out of their ears and noses.

This cartoon from 1918 shows the flu as a giant monster.

Flu patients could get fevers as high as 105°F (40.5°C). Some coughed so hard that they tore their stomach muscles.

Some flu patients had extremely high fevers that caused them to become **delirious**. They became so dizzy that they could not stand or even talk clearly. One of these flu sufferers in Virginia thought his crying baby daughter was a wildcat attacking his family. He almost threw the baby into a stove fire. Luckily, his wife stopped him before he was able to harm their daughter.

In the worst cases, a victim's skin would turn purple or blue because the body wasn't getting enough oxygen. Death was just around the corner for these patients.

The 1918 flu strain weakened its victims' lungs. This often led to a lung infection called **pneumonia**. Patients who died from pneumonia stopped breathing as fluid slowly filled their lungs.

It took some flu victims weeks to die. Others died just hours after they began to feel sick.

# Trying to Stop a Killer

In 1918, there were no medicines to fight the flu and few medicines that could help patients with their terrible symptoms. There weren't even enough doctors and nurses in the United States to treat everyone. Many had been shipped to Europe to help wounded soldiers.

Often, people used home cures to treat or prevent flu infections. These included stuffing salt up one's nose and eating onions at every meal. Most of these treatments, however, did not work.

This 1918 ad tried to convince people that a germ-killing tablet called Formamint could prevent them from getting the flu. Unfortunately, the tablets didn't work.

In public, people threw buckets of water and **disinfectant** on sidewalks to kill germs left from people spitting. Many people in the United States wore cloth face masks. They thought the masks would stop them from breathing in the flu germs. Little did they know that flu viruses are so small that they can pass through cloth.

The man on the right is not being allowed on a streetcar because he is not wearing a face mask.

This sign warns people not to spit because they might spread the deadly flu.

Some local governments passed laws to help stop the spread of the flu. New Yorkers caught coughing or sneezing without covering their mouths could get a year in jail and a $500 fine.

# Reminders of Death and Disease

Many cities in the United States closed schools, churches, and other places where people could get infected with the flu. Still, more people got sick. Signs of death and disease were everywhere. Many families hung **crepe paper** on their front doors to **honor** a relative who had died.

All theatres **CLOSED** until further **NOTICE**

At request of *MAYOR*.

Theaters such as this one in Seattle, Washington, were closed to prevent the spread of disease.

Germany was the main country the United States was fighting against in World War I. As a result, many Americans believed an untrue **rumor** that Germans were spreading flu germs in the United States on purpose.

Unfortunately, there weren't enough **coffins** or gravediggers to keep up with the dead. A body sometimes lay in a house for days, causing an awful smell. In some areas, drivers took horse-drawn wagons to homes to pick up dead bodies.

Healthy people were terrified. Who would be next to get sick? Even those who did not get very ill could spread the flu. Some were too afraid to go to the store, talk to their neighbors, or even leave their homes.

In Philadelphia, so many people died from the flu that the dead were buried in mass graves.

# Young Victims

Usually, most people who die from influenza are very young children or the elderly. Their bodies are often not strong enough to fight the disease. The victims of the 1918 flu strain, however, were different. Half of them were healthy people in their 20s or 30s. The deaths of many young adults meant there were fewer people left to do the daily work. Garbage went uncollected. Mail wasn't delivered. Many businesses failed.

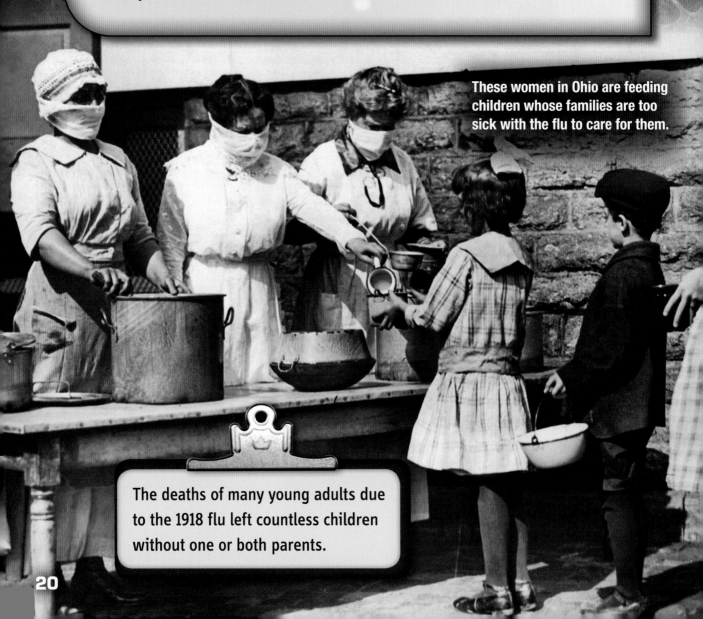

These women in Ohio are feeding children whose families are too sick with the flu to care for them.

The deaths of many young adults due to the 1918 flu left countless children without one or both parents.

No one knows exactly why the 1918 flu killed so many young adults. Surprisingly, some scientists believe that it was because young people have strong **immune systems**. The body's immune system may have overreacted to the flu virus, causing the body to fight too much and destroy its own cells. As a result, the immune system ended up harming the body rather than helping it.

Workers who came into contact with a lot of sick people, such as police officers and mail delivery people, had a high chance of getting the flu.

# A Lasting Impact

The 1918 influenza outbreak did much of its damage from late 1918 to the beginning of 1919. By early 1920, the pandemic was over. Most people in the world had been **exposed** to the virus. For many, their bodies fought off the disease. However, hundreds of millions of people did get ill. About 50 to 100 million of them died.

Until the outbreak ended in 1920, everyone from baseball players to barbers wore masks—even though they provided little protection against catching the deadly flu.

In the United States, survivors of the 1918 flu pandemic never forgot the effect of so many deaths. John De Lano was a boy when he caught the flu. He returned to school after he got better. Many of his friends, however, never came back. "I was a pretty lonely kid at the time because these were my friends that I played with all those years," he said, "and when I lost them, why, my whole world changed."

About 675,000 Americans died in the flu pandemic. The disease was much deadlier than World War I, in which 53,000 Americans died.

The 1918 flu spread to almost every place in the world where people lived—from Alaska to Australia to Japan. These Japanese schoolchildren hoped to avoid catching the flu by wearing masks.

# Help from Vaccines

Since 1918, scientists have learned much about treating influenza. Today, there are medicines that can fight the virus. There are also **vaccines** to help prevent people from getting the flu in the first place. If people take the vaccine before they are exposed to the virus, they will have **immunity**, or protection, from the flu. How do vaccines work?

Doctors suggest that people who are at a higher risk of getting the flu should get a vaccine every year. These people include those who have weaker immune systems than others—such as older people and very young children.

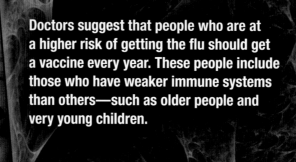

Some people don't get the vaccines and medicines they need to protect them from the flu. As a result, up to 500,000 people around the world end up dying from the disease each year.

Vaccines are a liquid and usually given as a shot. They are made of dead or weak viruses. The vaccine viruses don't cause real sickness. Instead, they protect a person by making them just a little sick, which causes a person's body to make lots of antibodies for that flu strain. If the strain ever enters the body again, the antibodies will "remember" it and easily fight off the virus.

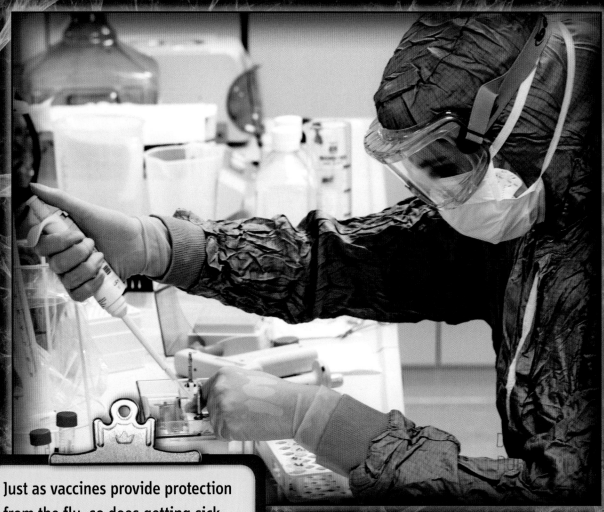

Just as vaccines provide protection from the flu, so does getting sick. A person who has had influenza will have immunity from that strain if it appears again in the future.

Flu viruses change over time. As a result, almost every year vaccine companies need to make new vaccines for the most common flu strains that are around at the time.

# A New Flu

Survivors of the 1918 flu pandemic have a connection to a recent flu outbreak. In 2009, a new flu virus sprang up in Mexico. It was a powerful strain. Just like the 1918 flu, the 2009 strain was more likely to damage a patient's lungs than the normal flu. In fact, the two strains are so similar that blood tests of 1918 influenza survivors showed that they had some immunity to the 2009 strain.

Scientists have named the 2009 flu that started in Mexico the H1N1 strain. It's also called the **swine** flu because it is similar to a flu virus that spreads among pigs.

A close-up of the H1N1 virus

This woman is spraying disinfectant on pigs to prevent the further spread of swine flu.

One 1918 flu survivor, Donald Jacobi, is now living in Canada. He has some advice about the 2009 flu. Although his doctor was wrong when he thought Donald would die more than 90 years ago, Donald still thinks the most important thing people can do is listen to their doctors. That is the best way to avoid catching the deadly disease.

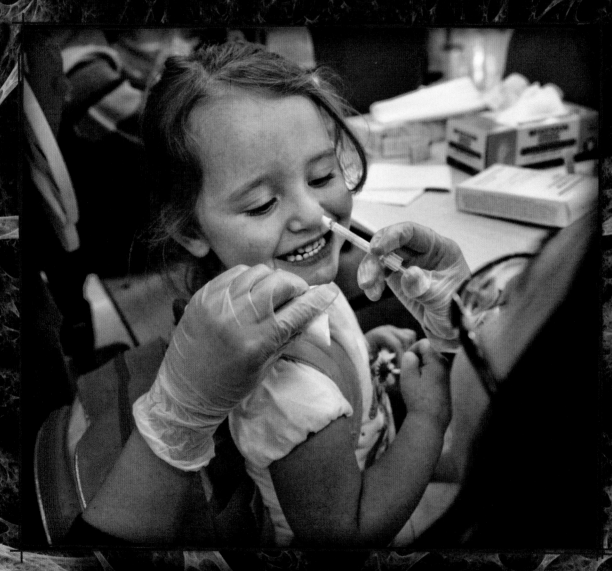

This girl is getting the H1N1 vaccine. Sometimes the vaccine is sprayed into a person's nose, as shown here, rather than given as a shot.

# Other Famous Flu Outbreaks

The 1918 pandemic was by far the deadliest flu outbreak in history, but there have been other recent flu pandemics that caused many deaths.

## The Asian Flu

- This pandemic started in China in February 1957. It spread to other parts of the world and reached the United States by June.

**Patients and medical staff pose for a picture in a Singapore hospital during the Asian flu pandemic.**

- Scientists created a vaccine for this flu in August. They called this strain H2N2.

- The flu reached its peak in the United States in late 1957. Many of those who became infected were schoolchildren. They caught the virus from classmates and then spread it to their families. However, most of the people who died from the infection were elderly.

- By early 1958, the pandemic died out. Between 1 and 2 million people were killed in the outbreak. At least 70,000 victims were American.

## The Hong Kong Flu

- This influenza outbreak began in Hong Kong in early 1968. It spread around the world and reached the United States in September.

- Like the previous pandemic in 1957, many people who came down with this flu were schoolchildren.

- This strain, which scientists called H3N2, was very similar to the flu virus from the Asian pandemic 11 years before. People who had been sick with the Asian flu had some immunity to the Hong Kong flu.

- The pandemic ended by early 1969. Because of the immunity some people had to the Hong Kong flu, as well as improved medical care, only around 750,000 people around the world died from this outbreak. About 34,000 of these deaths occurred in the United States.

**Many children missed school when they came down with the Hong Kong flu.**

# Flu Facts

The word *influenza* comes from a Latin word meaning "influence of the stars." Before people knew about germs, they thought flu outbreaks were caused by the stars. Here are some more facts about the flu.

## What to Do

- To avoid getting or spreading the flu, people should not touch their noses or mouths.

- Wash hands often with soap and warm water or use a hand rub made from alcohol. This will kill any germs.

- One should cover one's mouth with a tissue when sneezing or coughing. If there are no tissues, it is better to use a shirtsleeve than one's hands, which can get covered in germs and easily spread the disease to another person when they touch him or her.

- If sick with influenza, stay home. Don't go to school or other public places.

- In addition to the usual symptoms, some people with the flu may have diarrhea and vomiting. See a doctor if serious symptoms develop, such as trouble breathing or skin that is turning bluish in color.

- A person who was recently sick may still be able to spread the flu to others for a while after he or she starts to feel better. Stay home for at least a day after the fever goes away.

## Tracking the Flu Today

- The World Health Organization (WHO) identifies and keeps track of the most common flu viruses around the globe.

- Every year, the WHO makes recommendations to medicine companies about which vaccines to make.

- Flu viruses usually originate in farm animals like pigs or ducks. From there, a virus can change, or mutate, and spead to humans. Sometimes when a very powerful flu strain appears, many farm animals are killed in the area where the virus first appeared to prevent its further spread to people.

- Despite these measures, many scientists believe another huge flu pandemic is very possible in the near future. If it is as deadly as the 1918 flu, it could kill millions of people if a vaccine is not made in time.

Posters like this teach people how to prevent getting the flu.

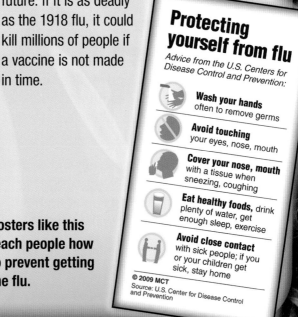

**Protecting yourself from flu**

Advice from the U.S. Centers for Disease Control and Prevention:

**Wash your hands** often to remove germs

**Avoid touching** your eyes, nose, mouth

**Cover your nose, mouth** with a tissue when sneezing, coughing

**Eat healthy foods,** drink plenty of water, get enough sleep, exercise

**Avoid close contact** with sick people; if you or your children get sick, stay home

© 2009 MCT
Source: U.S. Center for Disease Control and Prevention

# Glossary

**antibody** (AN-ti-*bod*-ee) a protein made by the body that attaches itself to harmful germs to stop infections

**cells** (SELZ) the basic, microscopic parts of an animal or plant

**civilians** (si-VIL-yuhnz) people who are not in the military

**coffins** (KAWF-inz) long boxes in which dead people are placed for burial

**crepe paper** (KRAYP PAY-pur) paper with a crinkled look and feel, used for decoration

**delirious** (di-LEER-ee-uhss) a state of mental confusion in which one may see things that are not real

**disinfectant** (*diss*-in-FEK-tuhnt) a chemical that destroys harmful germs

**exposed** (ek-SPOHZD) made open to possible infection by a disease

**fever** (FEE-vur) a rise in one's body temperature to a point that is above normal—98.6°F (37°C)

**honor** (ON-ur) to show great respect

**immune systems** (i-MYOON SIS-tuhmz) the systems that bodies use to protect themselves from harmful germs such as viruses that can cause diseases; they include white blood cells and antibodies

**immunity** (i-MYOO-ni-tee) the ability of the body to prevent infection from diseases, often resulting from vaccinations or a previous illness

**infections** (in-FEK-shuhnz) illnesses caused by germs entering the body

**influenza** (in-floo-EN-zuh) the flu; an illness caused by a virus; symptoms include fever and muscle pain

**invades** (in-VAYDZ) enters by force or takes over, usually in a harmful way

**microscopes** (MYE-kruh-skohps) tools that scientists use to see things that are too small to see with the eyes alone

**outbreak** (OUT-*brayk*) a sudden start of something, such as a disease among a group of people

**pandemic** (pan-DEM-ik) an outbreak of a disease that occurs over a huge area and affects a large number of people

**plague** (PLAYG) a disease that spreads quickly and often kills many people

**pneumonia** (noo-MOH-nyuh) a disease of the lungs that makes it difficult to breathe

**rumor** (ROO-mur) a story that is told by many people but has not been proved to be true

**swine** (SWINE) relating to pigs

**symptoms** (SIMP-tuhmz) signs of a disease or other physical problem felt by a person; often feelings of pain or discomfort

**unconscious** (uhn-KON-shuhss) not awake; unable to think, hear, feel, or see

**vaccines** (vak-SEENZ) medicines that protect people against diseases

**viruses** (VYE-ruhss-iz) tiny germs that can be seen only with powerful microscopes; they can invade cells and cause diseases

# Bibliography

**Barry, John M.** *The Great Influenza: The Epic Story of the Deadliest Plague in History.* New York: Viking (2004).

**Dobson, Mary.** *Disease: The Extraordinary Stories Behind History's Deadliest Killers.* London: Quercus Publishing (2007).

**http://1918.pandemicflu.gov/learn_more/04.htm**

**www.pbs.org/wgbh/americanexperience/influenza/**

# Read More

**Getz, David.** *Purple Death: The Mysterious Flu of 1918.* New York: Henry Holt (2000).

**Grady, Denise.** *Deadly Invaders: Virus Outbreaks Around the World, from Marburg Fever to Avian Flu.* Boston: Kingfisher (2006).

**Krohn, Katherine.** *The 1918 Flu Pandemic.* Mankato, MN: Capstone (2008).

**O'Neal, Claire.** *The Influenza Pandemic of 1918.* Hockessin, DE: Mitchell Lane Publishers (2008).

# Learn More Online

To learn more about influenza, visit
**www.bearportpublishing.com/NightmarePlagues**

# Index

antibodies 9, 25
Asian Flu 28

Boston, Massachusetts 12

De Lano, John 23
deaths 5, 11, 13, 15, 18–19,
    20–21, 22–23, 24, 28
doctors 5, 6, 8, 16, 24, 27, 29

Europe 11, 13, 16

face masks 17, 22–23

Germany 18
germs 8–9, 10, 16–17, 18, 29

H1N1 26–27
Hong Kong Flu 28

immune system 21, 24
immunity 24–25, 26, 28

Jacobi, Donald 4–5, 6–7, 8, 27

Kansas 10–11

laws 17
lungs 8, 14–15, 26

Mexico 26

Philadelphia, Pennsylvania 13, 19
pneumonia 15

remedies 16–17

soldiers 10–11, 16
Spanish influenza 11
spreading of flu 6–7, 8–9, 10–11,
    12–13, 16–17, 18–19, 21, 23, 26,
    28–29
symptoms 4–5, 9, 10, 14–15, 16,
    29

United States 12–13, 16–17, 18, 23,
    28

vaccines 24–25, 27, 28–29
viruses 8–9, 10–11, 12–13, 14, 17,
    21, 22, 24–25, 26, 28–29

white blood cells 9
World Health Organization
    (WHO) 29
World War I 11, 13, 18, 23

# About the Author

Jessica Rudolph has edited many books about history.
She recently learned that one of her great-great-aunts, an
Irish immigrant named Nellie Casey, died in the 1918 flu
pandemic while working as a nurse in New York City.